WEST FARGO PUBLIC LIBRARY
109 3RD STREET EAST
WEST FARGO, ND 58078

WITHDRAWN

D0857390

* Smithsonian

DESTINED FOR SPACE

Our Story of Exploration

by Don Nardo

CAPSTONE PRESS
a capstone imprint

J 629.43
N166

Capstone Press
1710 Roe Crest Drive
North Mankato, Minnesota 56003
www.capstonepub.com

Copyright © 2012 by Capstone Press, a Capstone imprint.
All rights reserved.No part of this publication may be reproduced in whole or in part, or stored in a retrieval system, or transmitted in any form or by any means, electronic, mechanical, photocopying, recording, or otherwise, without written permission of the publisher.

 Books published by Capstone Press are manufactured with paper containing at least 10 percent post-consumer waste.

The name of the Smithsonian Institution and the sunburst logo are registered trademarks of the Smithsonian Institution. For more information, please visit www.si.edu.

Nardo, Don, 1947–
  Destined for space : our story of exploration / by Don Nardo.
    p. cm. — (Smithsonian)
  Includes bibliographical references and index.
  Summary: "Describes the history and future of human space exploration"—Provided by publisher.
  ISBN 978-1-4296-7540-6 (library binding)
  ISBN 978-1-4296-8024-0 (paperback)
  1. Outer space—Exploration—History—Juvenile literature. 2. Astronautics—History—Juvenile literature.
I. Title.
  TL793.N348 2012
  629.45—dc23   2011031383

Editorial Credits: Kristen Mohn, editor; Sarah Bennett, designer; Eric Gohl, media researcher; Laura Manthe, production specialist

Our very special thanks to Dr. Michael J. Neufeld at the National Air and Space Museum for his curatorial review. Capstone would also like to thank Ellen Nanney and Kealy Wilson at the Smithsonian Institution's Office of Product Development and Licensing for their help in the creation of this book.

Smithsonian Enterprises: Carol LeBlanc, Vice President; Brigid Ferraro, Director of Licensing

Photo/Illustration credits: Alamy/Everett Collection Inc, 22 (top)/Universal Images Group Limited, 25 (top right) • Corbis/NASA, 22 (bottom)/Science Faction/NASA, 43 • Getty Images/Keystone, 6–7 (bottom)/Apic, 12/ Universal History Archive, 13 (top), 32–33/Paramount Pictures, 15 (bottom)/Hulton Archive, 16–17, 20–21 (bottom)/Time Life Pictures/NASA, 21 (top)/Fox Photos, 23 (bottom)/Time Life Pictures/Ralph Morse, 28 (left)/NY Daily News Archive, 29 (top right)/SSPL, 29 (back)/National Geographic/Bates Littlehales, 30/Space Frontiers/NASA, 31 (bottom) • The Granger Collection, NYC/ullstein bild, 19 (front) • Library of Congress, 6 (top), 16 (left) • NASA, cover, back cover (left & middle), 7 (bottom), 31 (top), 34 (all), 35 (top), 37, 38–39 (all), 45 (all)/Johns Hopkins University Applied Physics Laboratory/Southwest Research Institute (JHUAPL/SwRI), back cover (right)/ Marshall Space Flight Center, 26/JPL, 41 (bottom left), 47 (bottom left), 59 (right) • Newscom/Johann Brandstetter/akg-images, 13 (bottom)/ITAR-TASS, 20 (left)/Custom Medical Stock Photo/Educational Images LTD, 23 (top)/ RIA Nowosti/akg-images, 24 (right), 25 (top left), 28 (right)/UPI/NASA, 36/ZUMA Press/z03, 52–53 (front) • Photo Researchers, Inc/Dennis Milon/Allan Morton, 2–3/Astropics/Walter Pacholka, 6–7 (back)/Science Source, 7 (top), 27, 44/Sheila Terry, 11 (top)/Richard Bizley, 14–15, 57 (right)/Detlev van Ravenswaay, 24 (left), 49 (right)/Paul Wootton, 35 (right)/Mehau Kulyk, 40–41 (top)/Science Source/NASA, 40 (bottom left & bottom right)/JPL/NASA, 41 (bottom right)/Science Photo Library, 42 (top)/NASA, 42 (bottom), 46–47, 56–57/European Space Agency, 47 (bottom right)/David Hardy, 48–49/Julian Baum, 50–51 (all)/Victor Habbick Visions, 54/Babak Tafreshi, 55/David Parker, 58–59 • Shutterstock, cover (background & spine), 1, 4–5, 8–9 (all), 10–11 (back), 16–17 (background), 18–19 (back), 20–21 (background), 22–23 (background), 24–25 (background), 25 (bottom), 26–27 (background), 34–35 (background), 52–53 (back), 60–61 (all), 62–63, 64 • Wikipedia, 10 (bottom)

Printed in the United States of America in North Mankato, Minnesota.
102011   006405CGS12

Contents

Humanity's Greatest Adventure

> *"There is no way back into the past. The choice is the Universe—or nothing."*
>
> —H.G. Wells

The famous British science fiction author H.G. Wells said these words. He meant that humans can't return to the days when they knew nothing about the universe. Instead, they should reach out and conquer it. Like other great thinkers, Wells tried to picture people's future. He looked at our home, Earth. It appears huge to the average person. But Wells realized an important truth. Our planet is only a tiny speck in a vast universe.

Think of Earth as one grain of sand on a beach many miles long. The sand grains appear limitless. Similarly, the stars and planets in the universe seem countless. They are also mysterious and appealing. Wells believed that the human race is drawn to these points of light. In his view we have a grand destiny. It is to reach and explore those distant worlds.

Humans have long desired to see what lay beyond the horizon here on Earth. To find out, explorers braved incredible dangers. They climbed the highest peaks. They sailed across vast seas. They fought their way to the ice-covered poles. They even reached the ocean floors. In spite of the risks, they refused to give up. Many died along the way. Yet their deaths inspired rather than discouraged others. These efforts encouraged humans to explore still other frontiers. Gene Roddenberry, creator of the 1960s TV show *Star Trek*, famously called outer space "the final frontier."

But the fantastic dream of traveling beyond Earth is not new. It has existed for centuries. A few daring individuals in each generation imagined it. But they could not make it a reality. They lacked the know-how and equipment. Not until the 20th century did our abilities catch up with our dreams.

Explorers of the final frontier face enormous challenges. Space is an airless void. It is also filled with deadly radiation. Yet scientists and engineers found ways to overcome these dangers. In 1969 astronauts reached the moon. Soon after that humans launched satellites that flew by the giant planets Jupiter and Saturn. These vehicles zoomed at very high speeds. They also sent back stunning photos. They showed the surfaces of Saturn's moons in amazing detail and showed volcanoes erupting on Jupiter's moon Io.

These feats were remarkable. But they were only tiny first steps. A journey millions of times longer awaits. Many people, including most scientists, feel compelled to continue this great adventure. They are sure that humans will someday go to the stars. Neil Armstrong believes it. He was the first person to stand on the moon. To him, that moment was a crucial turning point. It showed that "humanity is not forever chained to this planet."

CHAPTER 1

Worlds in the Sky

Even before humans first considered traveling into space, the night sky filled them with wonder. They saw the sun set and the stars appear. They watched the moon change shape each month. Those changes are now called phases. People had no idea how those phases occur, but they were awestruck by them. We know this because of what was found in a cave in France. About 20,000 years ago, in the Stone Age, people lived in that cave. One of them drew the moon's phases on a rock wall.

Later generations of humans were also drawn to the sky. About 6,000 years ago, the people of what is now called Iraq studied the night sky. They tracked the stars' positions and divided them into groups. We call these groups constellations. Some were given the names of human characters. Others were named for animals or objects.

Over time these watchers—the earliest astronomers—noticed interesting things. First, the moon always moved through

the same 12 star groups. Together, these star groups became known as the zodiac. The watchers also noticed that a handful of bright stars moved slowly through the zodiac. These came to be called planets.

Each planet was named for a god. The brightest, for example, was linked to the goddess of love, Ishtar. Later the Romans called her Venus, which is the name that planet bears today.

Populated Planets?

Eventually some sky-watchers had an idea. Perhaps the moon and planets were other worlds like Earth. If so, maybe humans could someday travel to them. A few who were inspired by this notion were writers. They wrote the first science fiction stories.

One of these tales, titled *A True Story*, was written in about AD 160. The author, Lucian, was a Syrian who wrote in Greek. In his story a powerful wind lifts a group of people upward. The wind eventually carries them to the moon, which turns out to be inhabited. The travelers are surprised to learn that the moon people are at war. Their enemies live on the sun. The fight is over which race will succeed in colonizing another planet.

Another story of space travel came 14 centuries later. In 1611 German astronomer Johannes Kepler wrote *Somnium*, meaning "Sleep." It too describes a moon voyage. In this one demons carry the hero to the moon. They use drugs to put him to sleep. As Kepler tells it, the trip will take only four hours, but the traveler must move at high speeds. Only entering a sleeping state will keep him from being torn to pieces.

A bronze sculpture depicts Giordano Bruno's trial, in which he bravely defied church leaders.

The brilliant Kepler (standing) confers with Danish astronomer Tycho Brahe.

Paying a Terrible Price

One of the early writers who pictured populated worlds was Giordano Bruno, an Italian astronomer. He argued that the stars are other suns. Further, those suns have planets. Bruno also said that people might live on the planets. These ideas bothered the Catholic church's leaders. They felt this thinking went against certain passages in the Bible. For these reasons and others, Bruno was arrested and ordered to publicly admit he was wrong. He refused and paid a terrible price. In 1600 his captors burned him at the stake.

Gravity, Spaceships, and Martians

All of these stories had something in common. They featured imaginative ways of traveling in space. This was because science had not advanced very far. No one understood gravity. English scientist Isaac Newton was the first to describe it. It is an invisible force, he said. It holds people and objects on Earth's surface. In addition, it keeps the moon going around Earth.

Knowing about gravity unlocked a key for scientists. It allowed them to figure out something called escape velocity. This is the speed an object must travel to break free of a planet's gravity.

French writer Jules Verne was one of the pioneers of the science fiction genre.

Earth's escape velocity is 7 miles per second, or about 25,000 miles (40,000 kilometers) per hour. To make it into space, an object must reach that speed. Otherwise it will fall back to Earth.

More and more writers wanted their stories about space travel to sound believable. So they began to show ways of overcoming Earth's gravity. One was French writer Jules Verne. In 1865 he published his novel *From the Earth to the Moon*. It depicts a spaceship shaped like a big bullet. A huge cannon fires it into space.

Newton's Force

Isaac Newton was born in 1642. Before his time no one knew why objects thrown into the air fall back to the ground. A few thinkers suggested the cause was some kind of force. Kepler, for instance, thought it might be magnetism. Newton agreed that a force was involved. But it had nothing to do with magnets. He called the force gravity. Using math, he showed that gravity depends on mass. An object's mass is the amount of matter it contains. The larger the item, the stronger its gravity. Earth has enormous mass. Its gravity holds not just us, but even the moon in place.

Legend says a falling apple clued Newton in to how gravity works.

Martians attack London in H.G. Wells' *The War of the Worlds*.

H.G. Wells also imagined a way to defeat gravity. He used it in his novel *The First Men in the Moon*. The spaceship in the book is coated with a special substance that cancels out gravity's effects.

In *The War of the Worlds*, published in 1898, Wells imagined space travelers coming to us. In the story Mars has become too dry to support life, so the Martians decide to take over Earth. They arrive in large spaceships shaped like cylinders. These craft take advantage of gravity to land. Each glides in at an angle and crashes to the ground, creating a deep crater. From that pit, the invaders emerge.

Wells got the idea of Martian space travelers from public debates about Mars. In 1877 an Italian astronomer made news. He had been studying Mars through his telescope. He claimed he saw "channels" on the planet. By that he meant rivers. But the Italian word he used became "canals" in

English. Canals are built by people. So in the years that followed, an exciting idea began to spread. It held that Mars was inhabited by intelligent beings. Some people saw this as pure nonsense. Others argued that such aliens might indeed exist. The debates increased the planet's mystery and appeal. Since then the idea of exploring Mars has captivated many people.

Flights of Fancy

But how would people get to Mars? No one in Wells' day knew the answer. All space travel up to that time had been fictional. Such trips had been only imaginary. True, more than a century before *The War of the Worlds* was published, people had learned to float through the sky in balloons. But these were lighter than air. Balloons could only float as high as the air would take them, not into space. They also lacked power and proper controls. No human had yet come close to creating powered flight, in which people fly in craft that are heavier than air. Clearly, that kind of flight would require some sort of machine for power. Back then most people believed that building such "airplanes" was impossible. In 1901 *The New York Times* said it would take 10 million years to achieve human flight.

The first piloted balloon went up in Paris in 1783.

How wrong they were!

Just two years later, American brothers Wilbur and Orville Wright successfully flew a flying machine. The Wrights had started out building bicycles. Over time their eyes turned skyward. They and others built simple gliders. But these had no power source and no effective way to steer. That made gliders very dangerous. One daring German inventor died when his glider crashed.

The Wrights were saddened by that news. But they forged ahead. They ran many tests and trials. In time they devised a workable steering system. Next they needed a power source. So they asked mechanic Charlie Taylor for help. Together the three men pieced together a small

Orville Wright (piloting the plane) makes history at Kitty Hawk while his brother Wilbur watches.

engine that made their handmade propellers spin. This was it. They were ready.

The historic day was December 17, 1903. At Kitty Hawk, North Carolina, Orville Wright climbed onto the airplane. He flew it roughly 120 feet (37 meters) in 12 seconds. It wasn't far. But it was enough. The door to human space flight had begun to open.

CHAPTER 2

To Escape Earth

The Wright brothers and other inventors created a revolution in flight. Within just two decades, thousands of airplanes were built. Each year they flew faster and higher. Trips that once took weeks now took only a few hours. As a result the size of the globe seemed to shrink.

Not everyone was satisfied with airplanes, however. Those who dreamed about space travel realized that airplanes had limits. An important one was speed. Even their top speeds were far slower than escape velocity. So they could not break free of Earth's gravity. Airplanes had no chance of going beyond our planet's atmosphere into space.

Some people realized that only one device would do the trick. It alone had the potential to go fast enough to reach escape velocity. That device was the rocket.

People had known about rockets for a long time. The Chinese had built the first versions about 800 years before. They were small and primitive by modern standards. A person placed gunpowder in the rear section and ignited it with fire. The rocket sped upward, producing a flash of light and a loud noise. The devices were impressive but not very dangerous. They were not designed with space travel in mind. The Chinese used them mainly to frighten enemies in battle and Europeans used them for fireworks.

Early rockets were used in ancient China during battles.

WEST FARGO PUBLIC LIBRARY

Early Rocket Pioneers

A handful of forward-thinkers got to work on larger, better-built rockets. They hoped the rockets might go fast enough to escape Earth. Among these men was a Russian named Konstantin Tsiolkovsky. He was a math teacher who was interested in powered flight. He knew that rockets had much promise. He later wrote, "Probably the first seeds of the idea were sown by that great fantastic author Jules Verne."

The Russian knew that Verne's space cannon was unrealistic. But it made him think about rockets. He used advanced math to figure out rocket propulsion, the forward thrust a rocket produces. In 1903 he wrote the world's first scientific paper on space travel.

Tsiolkovsky also considered the concept of "step" or "stage" rockets. One rocket could go only so far. But extra power could be produced by adding more rockets. For example, he could connect two rockets to the first one. That would make a three-stage rocket. Each stage would fire in turn. The combined thrusts would cause the topmost stage to go much faster and higher.

Konstantin Tsiolkovsky

Robert Goddard shows off his liquid-fueled rocket in March 1926.

Another rocket pioneer was an American named Robert Goddard. Like the Russian, he thought about building rockets in stages. He also looked at the fuels then used in rockets. They were gunpowder and other solid explosives. These fuels were not powerful enough, he decided. It would be better to use liquid fuels, because they produce more energy when burned.

Goddard built the first liquid-fueled rocket using liquid oxygen and gasoline. Its test flight took place March 16, 1926, in Massachusetts. The device traveled 184 feet (56 m). Later, in 1935, Goddard launched a more advanced rocket. It traveled a total distance of 2.5 miles (4 km) from its launching point.

Goddard (second from left) with his four-stage rocket in Roswell, New Mexico, in the 1930s

Germany and Missile Weapons

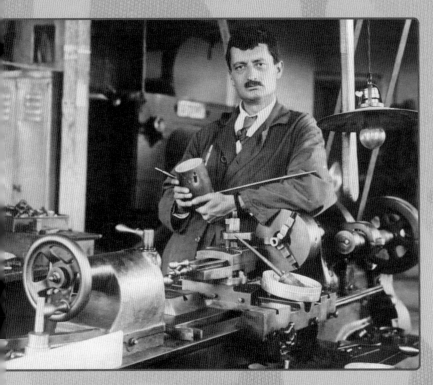

Hermann Oberth, photographed in his workshop, believed that humans could travel into space.

Germany's Wernher von Braun with a model of the *V-2* rocket

Hermann Julius Oberth was a third early rocket expert researching during this period. Like Goddard, he felt that liquid fuels were the way to go. Oberth wrote an important book about the liquid-fueled rocket. He was excited about its potential for flying into space.

Oberth's book prompted a lot of interest in space travel in Germany. In 1930 he carried out one of his first rocket experiments in Berlin. Assisting him was a brilliant young German student named Wernher von Braun.

Von Braun went on to form his own team of researchers for the German army. In 1934 his team launched a rocket. It made it to an altitude of 1.5 miles (2.4 km). After that the army poured more money into rockets. Army officers realized that they could be used as missile weapons. Von Braun designed a long-range rocket. Germany's Nazi dictator, Adolf Hitler, approved its use in 1942, during the height of World War II. The Nazis called it their *Vengeance Weapon 2* (*V-2*). The main targets were two of Germany's enemies, Britain and Belgium. Hitler's *V-2*s began falling on London in September 1944. The rockets did not secure a Nazi victory, however. Germany surrendered months later and rocket technology was soon put to better use.

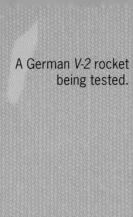

A German *V-2* rocket being tested.

A German *V-2* rocket caused devastation in London in 1945, not long before the end of the war.

The Race for Space

Germany's rocket program shut down at war's end. At that point the U.S. government saw an opportunity. It wanted to conduct the same kind of research, so it recruited Wernher von Braun and members of his team. Along with American engineers, von Braun built bigger, more accurate missiles. In 1949 the program produced the first multistage rocket. Its first stage was a modified *V-2*. Above it was a second, smaller rocket. It reached an amazing height of 248 miles (400 km) before falling back to Earth.

The Americans thought they led the world in rocket research. But they were wrong. The Soviet Union also took German ideas. Soviet scientists and engineers had been secretly working on rockets. By the late 1950s, they were ahead of the U.S. program in rocket power. As a result they soon shocked the world. In October 1957 the Soviets launched the first human-made satellite.

An early American *V-2* rocket nears its launch in White Sands, New Mexico.

A Soviet scientist makes last-minute changes to the *Sputnik 1* satellite.

The Soviets called their spacecraft *Sputnik 1*. Weighing just 183 pounds (83 kilograms), it was small, but it was fast. It orbited Earth once every 90 minutes. This was an amazing feat, but *Sputnik 2* was even more stunning. It carried a dog named Laika. For the first time, a living creature had made it into orbit around Earth. These spectacular accomplishments amazed and frightened Americans. If the Soviets were capable of this, what else might they do?

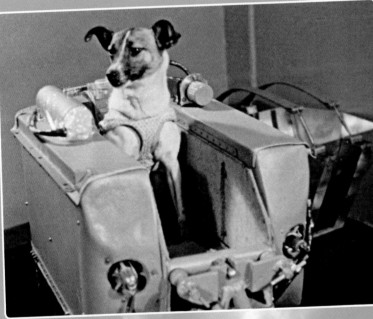

The space dog Laika (left) awaits its historic ride into space atop a huge Soviet rocket (above).

Going into Orbit

Sputnik stunned the world by going into orbit. When an object achieves Earth orbit, it strikes a balance. It is traveling fast enough to keep the planet's gravity from pulling it back down. But it is not fast enough to keep going outward into space. So it continues to circle Earth. Objects that orbit other objects are called satellites. Earth is a satellite of the sun. Natural satellites moving around planets are called moons.

U.S. leaders were alarmed. They were upset that the Soviet Union was ahead in space technology. American engineers now came under pressure to catch up. In December 1957 they tried to launch their own satellite. But the rocket blew up on the ground. In January 1958, however, they were successful. They fired the first U.S. satellite, *Explorer 1,* into orbit.

The contest to get satellites into orbit made one point crystal clear. The Americans were in an unofficial space race with the Soviets. U.S. officials felt there was no option but to win. So later in 1958 they took a vital step. They created an agency to handle space launches for peaceful purposes. They named it NASA—National Aeronautics and Space Administration.

The first satellite successfully launched by the United States, *Explorer 1,* blasts off.

A new shock for the Americans came April 12, 1961. On that day the Russian Yuri Gagarin became the first human in space when he orbited Earth once and returned safely. Six weeks later President John F. Kennedy stood before Congress. The nation should set a major goal, he said. Further, it should be met "before this decade is out." That goal was to land a person on the moon. No other feat, he said, "will be more impressive to mankind."

The pride of both countries was now on the line. Each set out to be the first to reach the moon. People around the world took notice. Some felt it could never be done. It was nothing more than a pipe dream, they said. But others were inspired and elated. Perhaps, they thought, a dream that had fascinated humanity for thousands of years might soon come true.

An American newspaper reports on Soviet cosmonaut Yuri Gagarin's record-making orbital flight. Cosmonaut is the Russian term for astronaut.

CHAPTER 3

Small Steps and Giant Leaps

The portion of the space race most in the news occurred between 1957 and 1969. At first the Soviets were well ahead. They followed up their *Sputnik* satellites with others. *Lunik 2* crash-landed on the moon late in 1959. Because the craft was so small and far away, no one on Earth could see the crash, even through telescopes. Scientists think the mini-collision carved out a small crater, adding to the millions of others scattered across the moon's surface. No dogs or other living things were aboard *Lunik 2*. But it was the first human craft to reach another world. A month later the Soviets scored another first. *Lunik 3* snapped photos of the moon's far side. Because the near side of the moon always faces Earth, the photos were humans' first glimpse at the mysterious far side.

The Russians continued to excel. In addition to the launch and successful orbit of Yuri Gagarin in 1961, the Soviets achieved other milestones. They sent two spacecraft carrying people into space at the same time in 1962. And in 1963 they launched the first woman into space.

These successes concerned many Americans. They worried about being so far behind in the space race. As time went on, however, worries began to fade. The United States rapidly made up for its slow start. In May 1961 NASA launched *Freedom 7*, piloted by astronaut Alan Shepard. The craft spent several minutes in space. The Americans were catching up.

A time-lapse photo of the Soviet craft Lunik 3 orbiting the moon

Valentina Tereshkova became the first woman in space in 1963.

Freedom 7 readies for launch.

DAILY NEWS
NEW YORK'S PICTURE NEWSPAPER®

5¢

"WHAT A RIDE!"

He's Up, He's Down, He Wins!

First Fotos of Spaceman Shepard's Pickup at Sea

The Moon Missions

Alan Shepard's mission was the first of six in NASA's Mercury program. Each craft carried a single man. One of the program's goals was to put a person into orbit. Another was to return him safely to Earth. Both of these goals were met even though there was considerable danger involved.

In the return phase, for example, the craft, called a capsule, plunged downward through the atmosphere. As it did, air particles smashed into it so fast and hard that it heated up and began to glow. Only a special evaporating material called a heat shield kept it from burning up. Eventually the craft used parachutes to slow its fall. Then it splashed into the ocean, sending a plume of water high into the air. A nearby ship was waiting to pick up the capsule and its pilot.

NASA named its next program Gemini. Each capsule in the program carried two men. The main goal was to spend up to two weeks in orbit. Another goal was for the astronauts to become experts at docking, which is connecting one capsule with another.

A Mercury capsule plunges into the ocean after a test flight.

In 1965 *Gemini 7* floats high above Earth.

U.S. *Gemini 5* astronauts C. Gordon Cooper and Charles Conrad Jr. meet with Navy divers minutes after their 1965 splashdown.

"That's one small step for a man, one giant leap for mankind."

Apollo, the final U.S. program in the space race, had the ultimate goal—to put a man on the moon. Each capsule carried three astronauts. In 1967 the three men in the Apollo 1 capsule died in an accidental fire during a ground test. They were the first three of the 21 American and Russian space travelers who have died in their spacecraft. At NASA and around the United States, people said that despite the terrible tragedies, the program must go on.

The Apollo program did go on with great success. On July 19, 1969, Apollo 11's main craft, the *Columbia*, went into lunar orbit. Aboard was astronaut Neil Armstrong. With him were Edwin "Buzz" Aldrin and Michael Collins. The next day Armstrong and Aldrin climbed into the attached landing craft, the *Eagle*. The lander separated from the main capsule. While Collins stayed behind to pilot the still-orbiting *Columbia*, the *Eagle* descended. A few hours later, Armstrong spoke the famous words, "The *Eagle* has landed."

Armstrong climbed out. As he stepped onto the powdery surface of the moon, he spoke 12 historic words to a waiting world: "That's one small step for a man, one giant leap for mankind."

After this triumph NASA launched six more moon missions. In all, 12 Americans walked on the moon. The missions were considered a tremendous success, in part because through them the United States won the space race. Also, the missions gathered many samples. The astronauts brought back 841 pounds (381 kg) of moon rocks. The samples revealed much about the moon's makeup. They also showed the age of the solar system and provided clues as to how it formed.

In addition, the astronauts did more than 60 tests on the moon. In one test they placed special mirrors on its surface. Scientists on Earth later bounced laser beams off the mirrors. This gave an amazingly precise measurement for the distance between Earth and the moon. That distance averages about 238,857 miles (384,403 km). The mirrors indicate that the orbiting moon is moving away from Earth by 1.5 inches (3.8 centimeters) per year.

Driving a lunar rover, U.S. astronaut Eugene Cernan passes by the Apollo 17 lunar module.

During the Apollo 17 mission, astronaut Harrison Schmitt scoops up samples from the moon's surface.

Among the samples collected in the Apollo 15 mission was one nicknamed the "Genesis Rock."

Astronaut Schmitt works beside a huge boulder on the moon.

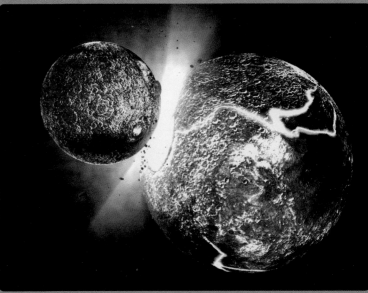

The Big Whack

The Apollo moon missions collected huge amounts of data about the origin of Earth's natural satellite. After studying this information, scientists found that the moon was born about 4.5 billion years ago. This was not long after Earth itself had formed. One day an object the size of Mars—about half the width of Earth—smashed into our planet with incredible force. Experts nicknamed the collision the "Big Whack." The Earth absorbed much of the object. But large pieces of both bodies splashed away into space. They went into orbit and over time they cooled. As more time passed, gravity went to work. It eventually pulled the separate pieces together into a ball—our moon.

The First Space Stations

People across the globe hailed the Apollo program. Yet most realized it was only one step in the great journey into space. The Americans, Soviets, and others went forward with the next steps. One was to create space stations in Earth orbit. Astronauts and scientists would live and work in these stations. They would stay for weeks or even months. The goal was to learn how to live in space for extended periods. This was necessary to future steps, such as creating industries in space. Another planned step is to build colonies on the moon and Mars.

The U.S. Skylab 1 space station orbiting high above our planet in 1974.

Carried by its two huge rocket boosters, the space shuttle *Atlantis* zooms upward in 1992.

Building orbiting space stations began in 1971. The Soviets put the first space lab, Salyut 1, into orbit. It circled Earth at a height of 186 miles (300 km). The Americans created their own station, Skylab, in 1973. It orbited at 270 miles (435 km). The Skylab crew carried out many studies. Some looked at how long periods in space affect the human body. They also took photos of Earth. Some of these studies increased our knowledge of weather patterns. Others showed forest growth and losses.

In 1981 NASA began the space shuttle program. A shuttle looked like an airplane attached to a large fuel tank and two rocket boosters. On the way to orbit, a shuttle threw away the tank and boosters. After that it had two jobs. First it served as a small space station. Its crew carried out many tests. The other job was to act as a "space truck." Most shuttles carried satellites and other objects into orbit. Later, when a shuttle returned to Earth, it landed on a runway like an airplane.

More and bigger space stations followed. One was the Soviets' Mir, which operated from 1986 to 2001. Largest of all is the International Space Station (ISS). Sixteen countries fund it. They include the United States, Japan, and Canada, along with the member countries of the European Space Agency. Russia, part of the former Soviet Union, is also a member of the ISS. Instead of competing, the United States and Russia began to work together after the Soviet Union separated into independent states.

Like Mir, the ISS was built piece by piece. Each section is called a module. The first module was in orbit by 1998. More modules and equipment were added over time. The station was finally completed in 2011. Much research and testing takes place on the ISS. Some of it involves finding new medicines to cure disease. Related studies include bone growth, human genes, and better vaccines. The crew also researches clean energy, robots, and radiation in space. In all, studies done aboard the ISS number more than 1,000.

The Mir Space Station

The Soviets launched Mir in 1986. They planned to maintain it for five years, but it lasted 15. During those years it sped around Earth 86,325 times. The station orbited at a height of 250 miles (400 km). Some people said it looked like a huge dragonfly. An American astronaut put it another way. He said it was like "six school buses all hooked together." That astronaut was one of seven Americans who worked on Mir. U.S. space shuttles began docking with it in 1995. Over the years the Americans and their hosts conducted about 23,000 tests on the space station. In one they oversaw the first wheat crop grown in space. This was important partly because it showed that in the future, space colonists will be able to grow their own food.

The U.S. space shuttle
Endeavour docked to the
International Space Station
in May 2011

Mariner 2 blasts off on August 27, 1962, bound for Venus.

Scientists prepare Mariner 4 for its 1964 journey to Mars.

Probes to the Planets

Building orbiting stations was a major task. But it was not the only goal space scientists pursued. The second was to begin exploring the rest of the solar system—the sun's family of planets, moons, comets, and other orbiting objects. It was clear that using human pilots would be dangerous. It would also be very complex and costly. So scientists settled on satellites and robotic probes.

Flights of these probes began even before the moon landings. NASA's Mariner 2 flew past Venus in 1962, showing that the planet's surface is extremely hot. Mariner 4 flew by Mars in 1965. Later, in 1971, Mariner 9 made history in another Mars mission. It became the first Earth craft to orbit another planet. These and other probes took many photos. The Mars pictures showed moonlike craters on its surface. They also showed volcanoes bigger than those on Earth, revealing that Mars and Earth have common features.

Mariner 4 snapped a photo of a cluster of craters on Mars' surface in July 1965.

Mariner 9 took a photo of Mars in November 1971.

The next step was to send landers. Their job was to explore the planets' surfaces. They would snap photos and test temperatures. The Soviets placed several landers on Venus in the 1970s. They found a poisonous atmosphere. The air was laced with acid and was hotter than a furnace.

The probes were destroyed only minutes after landing—but not before they were able to send radio signals carrying data back to Earth. Meanwhile, NASA put two landers on Mars in 1976. They collected soil samples. Small onboard labs tested the samples. No traces of life were found.

A Viking lander (left) rests on the surface of the red planet, Mars, in 1976.

The long white beam from the Viking lander (below) holds sensors that measure wind speed, air temperature, and more.

Later probes flew by the four giant planets. They confirmed an existing theory that Saturn's rings are made of billions of small chunks of rock and ice. Faint rings were found around Jupiter and Uranus too. Dozens of new moons were discovered. And giant storms were seen on Neptune. Human understanding of the universe was growing by leaps and bounds. Even more thrilling was the knowledge that there is still so much more to discover.

Saturn, with its majestic ring system, looms large in a photo taken by the Voyager 2 spacecraft.

CHAPTER 4

The Solar System and Beyond

The great spiral galaxy M81, lying
12 million light-years away, resembles
our own galaxy, the Milky Way.

The late 1900s were a thrill ride for space buffs. They witnessed one breathtaking stride after another. Dozens of space probes blasted off. They raced outward at incredible speeds. By 1989 probes had reached all the planets in our solar system.

As time went on, Mir and the ISS continued to circle Earth every few hours. One space shuttle after another docked with the ISS. The station kept expanding. In 1990 another fabulous device was put into orbit by a space shuttle—the Hubble Space Telescope (HST). This powerful telescope has taken thousands of amazing photos of the universe. The photos show stunning views of exploding stars and galaxies spinning at tremendous distances from our solar system. HST has even shown far-off galaxies colliding into one another.

These and other achievements showed our remarkable progress in understanding space. But they were only the bare beginnings of human space travel. Later more advanced probes were built that promise to go farther, faster, and send home even more information. Even better ones are on the drawing boards to power future discoveries. In time, experts say, we will go past the solar system's edge and head for the stars.

Two galaxies collide at a distance of 60 million light-years from Earth.

Enormous pillars in a distant region of space are composed of dust and gases.

45

Advanced Probes and Moon Bases

Reaches Jupiter in 2007

Leaves Earth in 2006

The New Horizons spacecraft is expected to reach Pluto in 2015.

In 2004 an advanced probe named Cassini reached Saturn. It began orbiting the ringed planet. Onboard sensors saw lightning flashes 1,000 times bigger than those on Earth. They also found eight new moons. Cassini flew by some of those moons and in 2005 sent a European lander, Huygens, to the largest moon, Titan. The lander studied the moon's thick atmosphere. It also found rain, lakes, and seas. All seem to be made of methane, a substance used as a fuel on Earth.

NASA's New Horizons probe is even more ambitious. In 2006 it left Earth for the dwarf planet Pluto. That tiny world lies 3 billion miles (4.8 billion km) from the sun. It is extremely cold there. Most of Pluto's atmosphere has frozen into ice and lies on its surface. New Horizons will reach Pluto in 2015. It will answer many questions about the dwarf planet and its three moons.

Unmanned probes will not be the only craft used in future exploration. Soon humans will return to space. And this time it may be to stay.

Space colonies will be established on the moon. Colonists will mine the moon's soil

New Horizons craft

Reaches final destination, Pluto, in 2015

The Cassini probe took a picture of Saturn's largest moon, Titan.

and rocks for minerals. They will be used to make building materials. That way the bases will steadily expand in size. Life-giving water will not have to be brought from Earth. In 2009 a probe found water on the moon in the form of ice, hiding in the shadows of craters.

The Huygens lander photographed Titan's surface.

The moon bases will pay off in many ways. First they will carry on valuable research. Also, resources from the moon will be sent to Earth. Finally, lunar mines will provide materials to build other space colonies. No rockets will be needed to get supplies off the moon. This will be done using clever devices called mass drivers.

In an artist's conception, Earth looms in the distance above a future lunar base. The long tracklike device is a mass driver.

An artist's rendering of a specialized mass driver that fires a payload at high speed from the surface of an asteroid

Cheap, Efficient Mass Drivers

Rockets are expensive to build and fuel, but they will not always be needed on the moon. There, gravity is weaker than on Earth, so mass drivers will be able to launch things. Miners will put materials, called the payload, in a bucket. They will then put the container on a long metal track. Strong magnets will make the bucket move faster and faster along the track. At the end it will fly off at great speed and go into orbit. Finally, a space truck will capture the bucket and carry it to the intended work site in space. Mass drivers may be used to mine large asteroids too.

Mars and the Asteroids

Beyond the moon, other science bases will likely be built. The next possible target is much more distant. It is the so-called red planet, Mars. Building bases on Mars will not be easy. Most importantly, a solution to the radiation danger on Mars will need to be found.

Further, just getting there will require major effort. Even when its orbital path brings it closest to Earth, Mars is still 150 times farther from Earth than the moon is. A trip to Mars will take at least several months, and flying humans there will be very costly.

Still, such a project may be doable with existing technology. The first few missions would indeed be expensive. But the cost would go down over time. This is because Mars has many usable resources. They include minerals and metals to build with. There is also hydrogen to fuel power sources. In addition, frozen water has been found on Mars, which humans could thaw and use. So new colonies could be built mostly with on-site materials.

In the future rockets could tow a water-bearing comet toward Mars to increase its water supply.

Remaking Mars

Some experts believe there's another way to colonize Mars. They say humans should terraform it. That is, they should make the planet more like Earth. First, people would find comets that contain water and crash them into Mars. That would increase the planet's water supply. Scientists could also use that water to create oxygen to breathe. Meanwhile, the colonists would release various gases now trapped in the soil. Over time the air would become thicker and slowly warm up. People would no longer need space suits. Such a project would take a long time and be very costly. Yet many people think it will happen someday.

A huge greenhouse on Mars could grow plants to be used to terraform the planet.

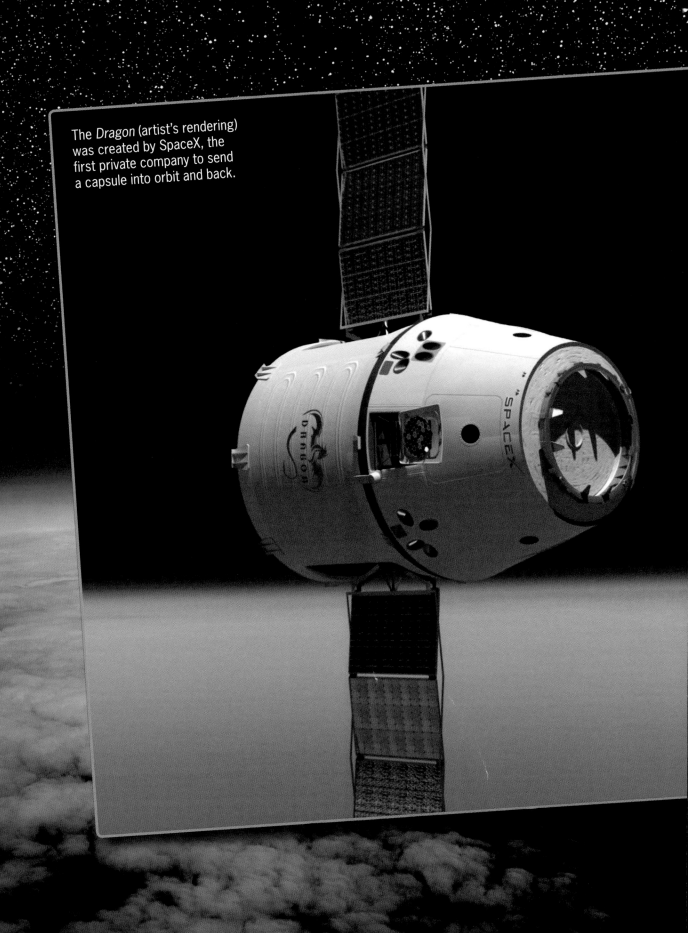

The *Dragon* (artist's rendering) was created by SpaceX, the first private company to send a capsule into orbit and back.

Touring Space

More than 500 humans have made it into space. Most of them have been astronauts or other professionals with years of training. But what about the rest of us? Will average citizens ever get the chance to travel into space? This idea of space tourism has been developing for many years. It will allow ordinary people a chance to take an other-worldly vacation.

Private aerospace companies are already building spaceships that fly tourists into space and back. These flights allow tourists to experience the strange but exciting feeling of weightlessness. A few wealthy citizens have already taken even longer trips to space. The Russian Space Agency has flown individuals on 10-day trips to the International Space Station. Many countries, including the United States, felt it was unwise to take untrained people into space. But the high cost the space tourists pay for these trips—$20 million or more—has helped fund Russia's space program.

Someday there may be other places to stay during a visit to space. Aerospace companies are building special space modules. These are private, orbiting vehicles that may be rented by space tourists. Small countries wanting to train astronauts and organizations planning to conduct research in space may also end up renting these vehicles.

In the future astronauts will not be the only ones going to space. As our understanding of space grows, the costs of the technology required to get there will come down. There will be more and more opportunities for all kinds of people to experience the thrill of a trip into space.

Drawn to the Stars

In these ways humans are venturing into our solar system. Yet in time they'll want to go farther. Some people already dream about interstellar travel. This will be the biggest challenge yet. Even the nearest star, Alpha Centauri, is very far away. Light moves at the fantastic speed of 186,000 miles (300,000 km) per second, and it takes more than four years for the sun's light to reach that star. Unless we can develop spaceships that approach the speed of light, it would take thousands of years for space travelers to get there from Earth.

How could a human ever live long enough to make such a trip? One idea is that the travelers could hibernate. They could go to sleep for a long time, and an onboard computer would wake them when the time was right. Another popular idea is to use a "generation ship." Miles long, it would be a huge space city. One generation of travelers after another would live and die on the trip. Centuries later their great, great (and many more greats!) grandchildren would reach the target star.

No one can say when or if such trips will become reality. But some people are sure they will. Humans once dreamed of flying like birds, they point out. In time they did so and went far beyond. Still, we are enchanted by visions of reaching the stars. As one noted space expert puts it, "Interstellar travel is the stuff that dreams are made of."

A generation ship would be large enough to have its own atmosphere, farms, and lakes.

Alpha Centauri is our nearest star after the sun. It would take thousands of years for space travelers to get there from Earth.

Alpha Centauri, the nearest star to our sun, is in the southern constellation of Crux, the so-called "southern cross."

Let Us Go Forward

In ancient times a few people dared to dream of space travel. But they had no idea if such a thing would ever be possible. In contrast, today everyone knows it is possible. Humans have stood on the moon. Probes from Earth have landed on other planets. A mighty telescope has shown us the universe.

But knowing that something can be done is not the same as wanting to do it. Some people question why others are so eager to explore space. They point out that many problems exist on Earth. These include war, hunger, and disease. It would be better, they say, to solve those problems first. Then humans might think about space travel.

But scientists and space buffs disagree. They argue that humans should aim for the stars. Going into space requires learning new skills, they point out. It also challenges people to build new kinds of technology. These advances benefit the entire human race. They help find new ways to grow food and cure diseases. And by giving all nations a common goal, space travel may help to eliminate war. The late science writer Willy Ley believed that. "A giant leap into space," he said, "can be a giant leap toward peace down below."

A Hubble Space Telescope image captures a cluster of stars lying 20,000 light-years from Earth.

Humanity's Mission

Some experts cite more crucial reasons to go into space. They say our survival depends on it. Earth has endured many terrible disasters in the past. Some were caused by stray asteroids that crashed into our planet. Powerful shock waves and giant fires killed millions of animals and plants. One such space rock struck Earth 65 million years ago. Its lethal effects wiped out the dinosaurs. People might someday suffer the same fate. This could be avoided, however.

Special satellites could stand guard in space. They would spot a possible threat when it was still far from Earth. Rocket engines or mass drivers would then nudge the object in a different direction, saving Earth from ruin.

No less important is finding life on other worlds. Simple life forms might exist even on moons in our own solar system or under the surface of Mars. NASA is already planning missions to Europa, one

Among other scientific pursuits, the massive Arecibo Radio Telescope in Puerto Rico searches for signals from extraterrestrial life in other star systems.

of Jupiter's larger moons. An ocean may lie beneath Europa's icy outer crust. It is possible that sea creatures exist there.

Intelligent life outside our solar system may also exist. Scientists are searching for it right now. The program is called SETI. The letters stand for the Search for Extraterrestrial Intelligence. Finding fellow thinking beings would be the most remarkable event in world history. We could exchange knowledge. That would enrich our understanding of the universe beyond measure.

H.G. Wells had such things in mind when he said "the universe or nothing." He meant that humanity must not stand still. For its own good, it must continue to progress—it must shoot for the stars.

One of Jupiter's moons, Europa, has an ocean beneath its icy surface. Many scientists think that life may have developed in those murky waters.

Timeline

c. 160

Lucian, a Syrian writing in Greek, publishes a story about a trip to the moon.

1600

The church burns Italian writer Giordano Bruno at the stake for saying that other inhabited worlds exist in space.

1611

German astronomer Johannes Kepler writes *Somnium*, about a moon voyage.

1642

English scientist Isaac Newton, who will explain the workings of gravity, is born.

1865

French writer Jules Verne publishes *From the Earth to the Moon*.

1898

British writer H.G. Wells publishes his novel *The War of the Worlds*, about Martians invading Earth.

1903

Russian Konstantin Tsiolkovsky suggests using rockets to send objects into space; Americans Wilbur and Orville Wright achieve the first powered airplane flight.

1926

American inventor Robert Goddard launches the first rocket that uses liquid fuel.

1944

During World War II, *V-2* rockets are first used against Britain and Belgium.

1957

The Soviets put the first human-made satellite, *Sputnik 1*, in orbit.

1958

The United States launches it first satellite, *Explorer 1*.

1961

Yuri Gagarin becomes the first human in space; U.S. President John F. Kennedy challenges the country to put a human on the moon by the end of the decade.

1965

U.S. spacecraft Mariner 4 flies by and photographs Mars.

1969

American astronaut Neil Armstrong becomes the first person to stand on the moon.

1971

The first space station, the Soviets' Salyut 1, goes into orbit around Earth.

1976

The U.S. space agency, NASA, puts two landers on Mars.

1981

The first U.S. space shuttle makes it into orbit.

1986

The Soviet space station Mir begins operation.

1990

The Hubble Space Telescope goes into orbit and starts snapping stunning photos of the universe.

1998

The first section of the International Space Station enters Earth orbit.

2004

NASA's Cassini Huygens spacecraft begins orbiting Saturn.

2006

The U.S. New Horizons probe is launched toward Pluto.

2009

A NASA probe finds water on the moon.

2015

The New Horizons spacecraft is scheduled to reach Pluto.

The U.S. Postal Service issued its first commemorative space stamp in 1948. Since then, the United States and many other countries have celebrated astronomy and space travel through postage stamps. The stamps are prized collector's items and honor human accomplishments in space.

asteroid: chunk of rock and metal left over from the solar system's formation; most exist in the asteroid belt, located between Mars and Jupiter

astronaut: a space pilot or traveler

astronomer: a scientist who studies space and the universe

capsule: a small craft that holds astronauts or other travelers

constellation: a group of stars in the sky that seem to trace the outline of a person, animal, or object

docking: the process of two spacecraft coming together

escape velocity: the speed an object needs to reach in order to escape the gravity of another object

extraterrestrial: coming from beyond Earth, or a being who originated beyond Earth

generation ship: a huge vessel or space city; many generations of space travelers will live and die on it as it journeys to a star

gravity: a force of attraction between objects; for example, the sun's gravity holds Earth and the other planets in orbit around it

hibernate: to sleep for a long time

interstellar: "between stars"; most often used to describe travel from one star to another

lunar: having to do with a moon

mass: the total amount of matter an object contains

mass driver: a device that uses magnets or electricity to throw objects from a planet, moon, or asteroid surface into space

module: an individual piece of a larger structure

orbit: to move around something, as when the moon orbits Earth

probe: a spacecraft sent to gather data

propulsion: the thrust or power that makes an airplane or rocket move forward

satellite: an object that orbits another object

solar system: the sun and all the planets, moons, and other objects that orbit it

star: a large heavenly body, like the sun, that shines by its own light

terraform: to transform a planet or moon in order to make it more Earthlike

universe: the total of all the space and matter known to exist

zodiac: the 12 constellations through which the sun, moons, and planets move each month

Select Bibliography

Albrecht, Mark. *Falling Back to Earth: A First-Hand Account of the Great Space Race and the End of the Cold War*. New York: New Media Books, 2011.

Friedman, Raymond. *A History of Jet Propulsion, Including Rockets*. Bloomington, Ind.: Xlibris Corporation, 2010.

Gamow, George. *The Birth and Death of the Sun: Stellar Evolution and Subatomic Energy*. Mineola, N.Y.: Dover Publications, 2005.

Getter, John. *To the Moon: Untold Stories of the Space Race*. Henderson, Nev.: Premiere Projects Digital Publishing, 2011.

Gorn, Michael H. *NASA: The Complete Illustrated History*. New York: Merrell, 2008.

Harland, David M. *NASA's Moon Program: Paving the Way for Apollo 11*. New York: Springer, 2009.

Zimmerman, Robert. *Leaving Earth: Space Stations, Rival Superpowers, and the Quest for Interplanetary Travel*. Washington, DC: Joseph Henry Press, 2003.

Zubrin, Robert. *The Case for Mars: The Plan to Settle the Red Planet and Why We Must*. New York: Free Press, 2011.

Find Out More

Helfand, Lewis. *The Wright Brothers*. Campfire Graphic Novels. Hanover, N.H.: Campfire, 2011.

Siy, Alexandra. *Cars on Mars: Roving the Red Planet*. Watertown, Mass.: Charlesbridge, 2009.

Sparrow, Giles. *Space Exploration*. Space Travel Guides. Mankato, Minn.: Smart Apple Media, 2012.

Wallace, Karen. *Rockets and Spaceships*. New York: Dorling Kindersley Pub., 2001.

Apollo 11 Lunar Surface Journal
http://history.nasa.gov/alsj/a11/a11.step.html

H.G. Wells' The War of the Worlds (full text)
www.fourmilab.ch/etexts/www/warworlds/warw.html

How Terraforming Mars Will Work
www.howstuffworks.com/terraforming.htm

The International Space Station
www.nasa.gov/mission_pages/station/main/index.html

Milestones of Flight: The Goddard Rockets
www.nasm.si.edu/exhibitions/gal100/goddard.htm

The Mir Space Station
http://history.nasa.gov/SP-4225/mir/mir.htm

Source Notes

p. 5, John S. Lewis. *Mining the Sky: Untold Riches from the Asteroids, Comets, and Planets*. Reading, Mass.: Addison-Wesley Pub. Co., 1996, p. 256.

p. 6, "Neil Armstrong Press Conference 1999." Space Quotes to Ponder. 18 Oct. 2011. www.spacequotes.com

p. 20, William Sheehan. *Worlds in the Sky: Planetary Discovery from Earliest Times through Voyager and Magella*. Tucson, Ariz.: University of Arizona Press, 1992, p. 20.

p. 27, John F. Kennedy, "Special Message to Congress, May 25, 1961." John F. Kennedy Presidential Library and Museum. 18 Oct. 2011. www.jfklibrary.org/Research/Ready-Reference/JFK-Speeches/Special-Message-to-the-Congress-on-Urgent-National-Needs-May-25-1961.aspx

p. 32, "One Small Step." Apollo 11 Lunar Surface Journal. 18 Oct. 2011. http://history.nasa.gov/alsj/a11/a11.step.html

p. 38, "Mir Space Station." Mir Space Station. 18 Oct. 2011. http://history.nasa.gov/SP-4225/mir/mir.htm

p. 54, Herbert Freidman. *The Astronomer's Universe: Stars, Galaxies, and Cosmos*. New York: Norton, 1998, p. 310.

p. 57, "Willy Ley." International Space Hall of Fame: 18 Oct. 2011. www.nmspacemuseum.org

Index

About the Author

In addition to his numerous acclaimed volumes on ancient civilizations, historian Don Nardo has published several studies of modern scientific discoveries and phenomena. Nardo lives with his wife, Christine, in Massachusetts.

WEST FARGO PUBLIC LIBRARY

4/2012